Poetry and Art

C Douglas Taylor
Poet

Catherine W Taylor
Artist

ISBN: 1481863290
ISBN 13: 9781481863292
Library of Congress Control Number: 2013900327
CreateSpace Independent Publishing Platform
North Charleston, South Carolina

Other Works by Catherine & Douglas Taylor

HOW TO PILOT AN AEROPLANE, (1973, 1974, 1978; revised edition 1986) *General Aviation Press*, humor, by C. Douglas Taylor, dedicated to Catherine.

FOOTBALL IN AMERICA, (2003), *Xlibris,* humorous novel by C. Douglas Taylor, cover art by Catherine Wright Taylor

DOWNTOWN DUCKS (2003), *Xlibris,* by Douglas & Catherine Taylor; children's story by Douglas; watercolor illustrations by Catherine.

THE REACTOR, (2008), *Xlibris,* novel by C. Douglas Taylor, cover art by Catherine Wright Taylor

THANKSGIVING, (2012) *Create Space.* by Douglas & Catherine Taylor, children's book; poem by Douglas, watercolor illustrations by Catherine.

Lighthouse Notes, (2001), a series of 24 greeting cards, combining Douglas's verse and historical notes with Catherine's watercolor paintings.

Acknowledgments:

We are most grateful for the invaluable aid and patience of: Mickey Bailey of Studio B Photography, Senatobia, MS for the photographic reproduction of the art works; to Roy Brewer of Memphis and the late Jack Abell for transcribing the songs.

In loving memory of

Helen Kressmann Taylor

POET

Preface

Catherine Wright Taylor, a native of Tennessee, is a graduate of the University of Tennessee at Martin with MFA from the University of Memphis. She studied art in college, drawing and painting in France, and sculpture in graduate school with Memphis sculptor Harris Sorrelle. She has directed the Oates Gallery in Memphis and taught art in the Shelby County Schools, the Saturday School of the Memphis College of Art, and Northwest Mississippi Community College.

Charles Douglas Taylor, a native of Oregon, grew up in Pennsylvania, was educated at Penn State, Gettysburg College, and the University of Florida. He has taught at eight different colleges and universities, including Westminster College, Christian Brothers College. Southeastern Louisiana, and Northwest Mississippi. His other works include the humorous aviation best-seller *How to Pilot an Aeroplane,* and two novels, *Football in America,* and *The Reactor.*

Catherine is a member of the *National Museum of Women in the Arts* and Douglas is a longtime member of the *Mississippi Poetry Society* Together they have produced a series of 24 **Lighthouse Notes** greeting cards and two other books, ***Downtown Ducks,*** and ***Thanksgiving*** each including her art work and his poetry or writings

Contents

CHRISTMAS CARDS

WELCOME HOME CARDS

The Artist's Brush

The Artist's Brush, like the artist's hand
Is but an extension of His plan
Who made the beauties of this earth
And everything therein of worth
And every scene we know in part
Is transfigured as a work of art
The artist's eye sees more than mine
Of all that's beautiful and fine
And as her hand the brush inspires
Another work of art transpires
And the brush's free and true invention
May be exactly God's intention.

2014

FIRST PLACE, RUTH RICHMOND AWARD
Mississippi Poetry Society 2014

DANCER, 2012, WATERCOLOR, 9" X 13"

Children's Poems

The Coats of Goats

There was an old goat named Billy,
Who said, "the whole world has gone silly,
Where people make coats
From the hair of their goats,
And the goats all go around chilly."

SECOND PLACE, POETRY FOR CHILDREN
Mississippi Poetry Society 1993

The Goat and the Frog

There once was goat
Who swam in the moat
Of a castle in Carmadee;

There was also a frog
Who sat on a log
Afloat in that moat by the sea.

Said the goat to the frog,
"You green bump-on-a-log,
Why don't you come swim in the water?"

Said the frog to the goat,
"You tattered old coat,
Don't you know you're a goat, not an otter?"

Horserabbits

There once was a rabbit
Who made it a habit
To serve horseradish each day.
His best friend was a horse
So often, of course,
He served horseradish and hay.

Thanksgiving

What do I have to be thankful for?
Possibly much, and probably more...
For friends I can talk to every day,
For things I can learn and games I can play,
For a dog or a cat or a house or a tree,
For a very best friend whose best friend is me,
For days full of sunshine, for days when it snows,
For ankles and elbows and fingers and toes,
For flowers and grasses and squirrels and birds,
For reindeer and bison and elephant herds,
To be thin or be fat, to be short or be tall,
For breakfasts and lunches and dinners and all,
For sisters and brothers and parents and friends,
For a new day that starts and an old day that ends,
For moonlight and starlight and twilight and dawn,
A chipmunk, a rabbit, a robin, a fawn,
For airplanes and rockets and trips to the moon,
For Christmas and Easter and April and June,
For whistling and singing, and the joy that it brings
To count all my happiest, favorite things;
I'm thankful for Love, and for all it can do,
I'm thankful for dreams and how they come true;
And I'm thankful that I can be thankful with you.

1984

COVER ART FOR THANKSGIVING, 2012, WATERCOLOR 6" x 6"

Humorous Poems

Capitol Briefs (2002)

(On the sighting of a fox entering the parking lot of the United States Supreme Court building in Washington DC, Wednesday, January 15, 2002. All occupants of the building were warned against touching the fox, if encountered, and a complete search of the parking building was undertaken. No fox was found. Neither was any record of a parking pass being issued to a fox.)

I

There once was a fox in a fix
Who came to the Court from the sticks;
When summoned, he sped,
But he said as he fled,
"I'm gone, but I've learned a few tricks."

II

Habeas Corpus Volponus
May have given the high court a bonus
For, when asked had he been,
He remarked with a grin,
"That is not my *probandi onus*"*

onus probandi [L., burden of proof]

THE GARDENER'S COTTAGE, OIL ON CANVAS 32" X 26"

The Collected e-mails of Who?

We have seen those collections of letters
In the libraries bound up in books
Full of secrets and bawdy confessions
So open, though nobody looks
The letters of J. Carroll Someone
In secret to Myrtle Mae Who
Her replies once the national scandal
Known now to a literate few

I propose as the key to my fortune
Or perhaps just to glory and fame
To gather up all the world's e-mails
Out of the great cyber-brain

To upload and download and store them
Their wisdom and insights profound
For children to read on their Kindles
As long as the world turns around

Now our thoughts can all be immortal
And when this world is destroyed
All our words, non-words and mis-spellings
Will live on in the lingering void

3ʀᴅ PLACE, PRESIDENT/VICE-PRESIDENT AWARD
Mississippi Poetry Society 2012

COTTON FIELD, WATERCOLOR, 2006, 13" X 17"

Our Hastening Ills

Oh well, or sick, or halt, or blind
We check our symptoms every day
While TV news and ads remind
It's medicate or pass away.

Lumbago, cancer, Parkinson's,
Kidney failure, failing lungs
Alzheimer's, arthritis, Atkinson's
Infect our bodies, minds and tongues

This syndrome or that, no matter,
We pick out one, or pick the lot,
Pass the symptoms, and the platter
Rehearsing daily what we've got.

'Tis the season for lumbago
Common cold, bronchitis, flu,
Down's the only way we may go
There's nothing else for us to do

The Springtime allergies with reason,
Help us stumble on downhill,
To the fearful sunstroke season
And onward toward the Winter chill.

They all come on, each in its time
Leading to that fated day
When good sense, or health decline
And we no longer have a say

Prepare for every ill or ague
Take the pill, endure the test
Do everything the wise men say do
Trust the doctors to know best.

Disease, disorder, our religions
Powerless, we wait our fate
And daily fill with our prescriptions
The gold and silver passing plate.

2012

Limericks

Scents of Mortality

I account it nothing but bunk
That the auto can vanquish the skunk;
Though it hammers his head
And leaves him for dead,
He lives from bumper to trunk.

SPECIAL AWARD: CONTEST CHAIRMAN'S DELIGHT
Mississippi Poetry Society 1993

Bumps in the Road

There's a certain lack of propriety
In living a life of anxiety;
If the road had no bumps
And the camel no humps
Then what would we do for variety?

2014

Filets of Soul
(Three high-church limericks
for David Lewis)

A minister of the Methodist edition
Had saved many souls from perdition,
But once in a while
He'd say with a smile,
"Lord knows, it's time to go fishin'."

A man of the cloth, not a rake,
Oft preferred angling to steak,
When a fishin' pal died,
He wept and he cried,
But he held the wake at the lake.

A man of the cloth, name of David,
Acquired the bass boat he crave-ed
Then, to save his shoes wear,
He would float everywhere,
Saying, "Think of the soles that I've save-ed."

Classified Limericks

(four limericks written on company time at
the Classified Advertising Department of the
Commercial Appeal, Memphis, 1986)

There once was a young Mary Ellen
A poet, to her way of tellin'
Her rhymes were so fine
They made the dogs whine
And set the bard's spirit to yellin'

There was a young lady Rebecca
Who hated to riska her necka
She wouldn't go flying
Unless she were dying
And her carpet was non-stop to Mecca

There was a young man, name of White
Who died by his bride in the night
She called Classified
To say that he'd died
And "Mr. Wright, write the right rite"

Memphis in May (Japan)

In the land where the sun is a-rising
They found the COMMERCIAL surprising;
They said "All this bad news,
It could drive you to booze,
But look at this fine advertising!"

1986

Early Poems

The Star in the Wind

There's a star in the wind
And the wind rides high
Through the cold and the dark
And the bitter alone.
There's a star in the wind
And the wind rides high
And the star in the wind is a word.

(1952)

Homecoming

on the farm at Gettysburg
June 15, 1962

It took a long time this time
Before the land felt fair and home
Beneath my native feet,
But it came, as it always comes,
And again I walked the land
And the land held me
And we were ours again.
And the day spent itself on night
And darkness took the distant hills
And still the land was mine...
I spend a pensive twilight then,
Rooted here, as my custom was
When all my days were young
And the land was mine indeed.

YELLOW TREE, 2012, WATERCOLOR, 10" X 14"

Southern Pine

Red leafed round in a warming wind,
Its brown-green needled limbs astir
In February's bland unseasoned breath,
Under a too-light snowless sky
That threatens little, promises less
It bends a brown bough, thoughtless,

While its brothers, ranked in Northland,
Sap-frozen, stiff, but living
Blue-green the snow-branched weight,
With brittle wind on frozen limbs
Know no promises of spring
Nor none believe, for there is time
Alone to clutch tight branch and hold – -
Not thought of spring or hope of morrow,
But steady place against the cold.

(1966)

"I Am"

In the beginning was the Word,
        and I said it
And later, since I hadn't heard,
        I read it

In the beginning was the Word,
        and I read it;
And later on, when I had heard,
        I said it.

(1975)

Space Flight

Beyond my ear and gone, it runs,
Beyond the tip of mountain rings,
Beyond the reach of time or sound,
In darkness still, beyond the night,
Across the ringing space it runs,

It spreads and thins and runs, out, out
By chance or charted accident,
Without propulsion now, or need,
On one unmeasured silent line,
Ever and ever, proceed, proceed...

But oh my God the wonder
If oh by God the chance
That somewhere in hurtling darkness lost...
The straight, straight line of flight conceives,
And then begins, by fractions,
That first minute infraction,
That slow, slight, inevitable curve, back, back...
Across the swelling ages, back,
Like some great blazing comet, back
Across the flaming skies.

All the darkness cannot quench the light;
All the silence cannot still that sound,
And though I in time lie down,
In my heart I turn, I know, I feel
The rush of that long sweeping arc
Through the far and flying darkness,
Which cannot help nor cannot slow
The timeless grace of that gathering charge.

(1975)

Bicentennial

And now to the truths we all hold dear,
A toast to the holy ringing year:
One red-white-and-blue can of lager beer
In memory of Paul Revere

(1976)

Poem in January

I take great care at the New Year's dawn
To write it right, from the first and on,
So early today at the head of a letter
On a machine unversed in timely matters
Except perhaps in terms of wear
I wrote the name of this good year.
The six, I thought, leave the five to heaven
But I strayed too far and struck the seven
And now upon the page I see
The impudent future laughing at me
Of months and years all out of rhyme
Making sport of life, of time;
I rub it out, I type it white,
But still I see, to it's delight,
The number knows somehow it's right.

(January 1976)

MADONNA IN BLUE ON BENCH, 2008

Power and Grace

For near-nine innings Neuhauser blanked the Yanks –
A hit here, a hit there, perhaps a walk,
But nothing a strikeout wouldn't mend.
Each time Dimaggio came to bat
The stadium trembled beneath the weight
Of cheers and hopes and hero-dreams.
The first three times he went down, easily,
Gracefully, while the crowd oohed and sighed;
And Neuhauser pitched on,
Safely, till the ninth.
His teammates from Detroit, or wherever,
Had gotten him a single run, and he clung
To that thin thread of a lead all night long
Toiling on the alien mound
Of the House that Ruth built..

    Two out,

    none on

    in the ninth --

Three more pitches and the victory shower:
Then Dimaggio doubled,

    Keller doubled,

    Henrich doubled,

And we all went home -- they to showers
Of Easy Victory and Hard Defeat -- and I
At age thirteen, to tell the tale
A thousand times, where I had been,
The wonders I had seen.

(1977)

Third Place, West Virginia Poetry Society Contest, 1999

Painting May-Pops
(Beth's Painting)

She kneels on the leaf-lawn forest floor
On an Easter April day
And paints in light and line and form
The first green hint of May

Her hair blows long in the wind of Spring
Her brown eyes deep in dreams
Her brush moves gently in the flow
Of all that is or seems

Her hand and brush conduct as one
Flowing of the wrist
A melody where Spring and sun
Are mingled with the mist

Overton Park
Easter, 1980

Family Poems

November Eighth

You stood there briefly on the brink as one,
A lad and a girl come fresh from Tennessee;
The bond conceived, as quickly tied and done –
One did not wait to wed in   '43....
Who could have known, or hoped, or even guessed
That knot would hold these forty-seven years,
And life survived become a life well blessed
With faith and trust and joy surpassing fears.
Again the date once more comes neatly round,
And once again the mem'ry traces back
Through smiling friends, sweet faces sought and found,
Who've gone apace along the earthly track,
While we who've shared the blessings of your hearts
Thank God for you and our companion parts.

(1990)

For Naomi Catherine Williams
May 31, 1993

Congratulations, graduate!
We think it's time to celebrate,
To put the books upon the shelf
And cheer, "You did it all yourself!"

So take some time to hear the cheers
Before you turn to face the years,
And when you set out on the road
May grace and wisdom share your load;

May all your grandest dreams come true
And grow to more, as dreams will do,
And when you reach the mountain's height
And see your burdens all grown light,

When you look back and pause apace,
May God shine light upon your face
And show you, as he surely can,
Your place within his master plan.

TREES, FRANCE, 1978, OIL 10" X 7½"

For the Carver of Roasts
Father's Day, 1994

Here is a little collection
For the sharpest host of all hosts,
The slicer of ham,
Or steak or of lamb,
But more often the Carver of Roasts.

When all the family is waiting
And the carving job has turned tough,
And your very best blade
Has left you dismayed,
One knife is just never enough.

So here, have an extra back-up,
And a back-up to back-up the back,
And if company drops in
And sits down with a grin
Guess who can take up the slack?

And now we've solved your dilemma
And we'll gladly solve others, but then
There may be an "edge"
To this humorous pledge;
You may have to feed us again!

Pawn to King One
(Father's Day, 1996)

Since today is Father's Day
We need a little verse
With all our hearts together,
But first we must rehearse:

I guess we ought to mention
Your years of strain and toil,
Of chasing black cows in the dark
And tilling the dark brown soil,

We praise the hand of providence
That kept you safe from harm
Through thirty missions in the war
And forty on the farm.

For God's not the only Father
That we would like to praise
And thank him for his blessings
That shine through all our days,

As we bow our heads and listen
To hear the blessing prayer
With thanks that we've come home again
And thanks that you are there.

For Sandra

Yes, times were hard when you were young
The weight of children, the labored years;
Now newer, heavier times have sprung
And brought these deeper, harder tears.

I see you there in my mind's hard toss,
Your family gathered all in grief
To bear somehow your helpless loss
Brave and battered in disbelief.

They seek the mother, friend, and wife
To console, the family font of strength,
Return to the deep well-spring of life,
The mother-lode that lends endurance length.

May, 1999

30th Birthday
(For Mary Lesa)

Now that you're thirty and have opened your eyes
We know that you must be astoundingly wise
So tell us at once, or when you have time
(that was thrown in for the sake of the rhyme)
Is it better, oh wise one, when all's said and done
To have one niece of thirty, or thirty of one?

(2003)

DANCING FIGURE # 1, 1981, BRONZE, 12"H
PURCHASED BY MARJORIE LIEBMAN, 1981

60th Anniversary
for Jim & Virginia

Sixty years of solid space
Loving toil and granted grace
Lead the hearts of those who share
In blessings known and unaware
To thank you from our deepest hearts
For sharing with us all your parts
And asking God when all is done
For a healthy, happy sixty-one.

November 8, 2003

For Allan The Elder
June 24, 2006

Happy Birthday zero-six
(If you do a number fix)
And some other little tricks
None will dare to tell you nix
Unless they're really bores and hicks

This is such a landmark year
The best one yet, we have no fear
So don't lament or drop a tear
Just do the things that you hold dear
Like put some sugar in your beer.

At the crack of noon, awake,
Give the party hat a shake,
Blow out the candles on your cake
Don't eat them lest your tummy-ache,
Or count them, that's a big mistake!
> Your pal,
> Bill Shakespeare

For Matt and Naomi
October 13, 2007

Hail the happy couple!
Hail the happy day!
Hail the friends and loved ones
Who send you on your way.

Matthew Hail! Naomi hail
We wish you life and love,
Godspeed on your journey
And guidance from above.

The course you plot is a handsome one
With many a port of call
But may you find your own home port
The safest of them all

We who stand upon the strand
Will watch you travel far
Two souls upon a wide, wide sea
Guided by one star.

Happy Birthday Mama

Happy Birthday Mama,
Virginia, and Mary V,
Of all the people that we love
You are our favorite three

We love you for the caring heart
You share with all in need
Your faith and generosity
That form the family creed

We love you for your guidance
And all the things you teach
By shining bright example
And have no need to preach

We love you for your patience
Which we've tried through the years,
In turn received your blessing
And had no need for tears.

We love you for your family
Well anchored in the storm
By faith, to give them courage,
And love to keep them warm.

2008

LITTLE DANCER, BRONZE 8½"H

Happy Birthday Maddie
May 14, 2010

Of all the flowers I ever see
The red rose seems most sweet to me
And of all the flowers that heaven knows
The finest must be Madeleine Rose
May the finest day for you and me
be Happy Birthday # 3

For Mary Virginia James Wright
on the occasion of her 90ᵗʰ Birthday

Happy Birthday, Mary V
From every person you can see
Gathered here from far and near
And all who hold you oh so dear,
We come, a clan that you know well
Each one with a tale to tell,
Daughter, grandchild, nephew, niece,
Cousins, in-laws, friends not least,
To lift a glass and share a plate,
To honor and to celebrate
With thanks to God and thanks to you
For all you've done for us and do
To help and guide us down the road,
To love and bless and share a load
And steer us by example true
To comfort us and feed us too,
And know whatever we might do
It could not match what you have done
To bless and nurture every one.

February 26, 2011

From Our Travels

Atlantica

It was, the guide book said, the best spot
In the quaint little coastal town
For sea food or the view.
We called ahead the day before,
So our reservations, or luck,
Or chance got us that good spot,
Second-best in the house, or out,
Just free from under the canvas cover,
With a view of the sky above
And most of Camden harbor
Two others had the best spot,
Further out, on the corner deck
With a clear view of all that lay beyond,
And the best site was the lady's;
The man, kindly featured, smiling,
Had taken the outside seat looking in,
Leaving the slender girl in blue
The inner seat with all the view.
Her dark dress bore flowers, bright red,
Her straight hair to her shoulders still
As her prim figure, her right hand light
And delicate on the stem of the glass
Of cold white wine; her alabaster face
Turned away from the harbor
Toward the sound of the waterfall
Rushing across the red-brown rock,
The people passing on the dock.

At her feet, to my surprise, a dog.
That would be no surprise in France,
But here, it was... I dropped my glance:
A black shepherd, quiet and still at her foot,
A dark green harness on his shoulders,
A sign: "Don't pet me; I am working."
He did not stir when her meal arrived,
Or turn, or alter our view of the water,
Of the schooners fast by piling and dock,
Of the slender fingers searching out
Each single seashell on her plate
To find it, to gauge it, and to know,
In the dark, how to manage all.

FIRST PLACE, FRANCIS P. DENINGTON MEMORIAL AWARD
Mississippi Poetry Society 2006

Tennessee Ballad

We walked the hills of Tennessee
My brother-son and I
Where new mown oaks had leafed the land
And branched the blue-blown sky;

We trod the valley new with green
And climbed the rocky slopes
Where water fell into the dell
And mists arose as hopes.

Upon the crest he paused to rest
A sweep of arm to show
Where he would see the cattle barn
The water pond below.

"I'll build my house upon that height
That none else can command
I'll set my name upon the gate
My title on the land.

Here fathered sons will come to rest
Their sons and grandsons too
To take their stand upon the land
Which I have walked with you."

In the Cotswolds, 2013, watercolor, 9" x 12"

I marked his words, his grazing herds
His hills and falling streams
And saw in grace his measured space
Against his fielded dreams.

(2008)

Honorable Mention, Gulf Coast Writers
Association Award
Mississippi Poetry Society 2013

Lines Composed
Upon Westminster Bridge
May 27, 1979

Let us have monuments to men
Who cleanly die for God and King
And send home neat remains, Amen,
O'er which the Abbey's matins ring

Forgive us Father, for well we know
Motives that drive to snare and pen
As your great work goes on below,
Helped in fits and starts by men.

Serendipity
for Pamela

Leaving, we reflect with delight
Upon two prayers launched in light
One for a place to spend the night
One for a guest who will fit just right
How God moves we can only sense
With shelter joy and recompense.
May every prayer you ever say
Bring blessings in the selfsame way.

Murski Homestead B&B
Brenham, Texas, March 22, 2003

Honoring Others

For Asher Tarmon of Israel
on his 90th Birthday

(November 25, 2009)

You are the man my praises sing
My near and distant hero-friend
My first in knowledge and esteem
Of nation-building, laboring men
Who see and launch and live the dream
That others then may come to know,
Whose hard sweat and spirit drive,
Enhance, sustain one land and all,
And keep the human race alive.

To rightly sing this birthday praise
Would take much more than I can do,
More voices, notes, and many days,
An earthly choir in Hebrew, Yiddish,
English, German, French, and more
Resounds from here to there to then
Stepney to Devon, Udine, Vienna,
Kfar Blum to Detroit to Tel Aviv,
From New York to Rio to Rome,
Around the world and back again:

Who has forged and thought and loved
And fought to bring his people,
Like Moses to the Promised Land,
Brave, destined land of hope and faith,

And there to bless that land with light,
Music and learning, and all the mind
Can translate for goodness sake,
Of all that good men needs must say
To give the vagrant world again its head
Lest generations pass and leave unsaid
What we have been and done, and what
We needs must do and be again.

In Memoriam
Bill Lipscomb

(for Rebekah, his mother)

Where do they end, a good man's days
Who lives on in a hundred different ways
Who lives in family, children, friends
And spreads to a thousand different ends
He lives in the deeds that others do
That mirror aspects that were true
In gestures, phrases, thoughts we knew
Of him, his one life here, a man
Well within the earthly plan
Of God, who knows and brings to pass
All we pick up, share, and pass,
Copy, add, and pass along
Like other stanzas in this song
Of life, building on the ones before
And passing on the same and more
Of love, and thought, and human worth
For one grand mission here on earth
Least known, least sought, nor understood
How all that's wrong is turned to good
We know but never comprehend
That all will tally in the end:
The way he does a kindly deed
The way she helps a friend in need
The way you take time for a chat

NEW OCEAN, 2014, OIL, 24" X 20"

The way a grandson wears a hat
A hundred dozen different ways
Remind us to our grand amaze
There is no end to a good man's days.

2002

Honorable Mentions: Mississippi Poetry Society
Joe Hutcherson Memorial Award, 2011 &
Herbert & Inez Shelton Memorial Award, 2012

*In Memoriam, W. C. H.**

Still stands the beacon on the coast

And guides the wandering bark,

And still, when passed and gone from sight,

Shines bright into the dark.

1990

*. W. C. Haley, colleague, Methodist circuit minister,
B-25 pilot in WWII.

For My Neighbor
(leaving for work at 6 a.m.)

There's more to life than labor;
There's less to life than love.
Should I dare to tell my neighbor
There's more to life than labor
If he's never seen Mt. Tabor
Or wears a workman's glove?
There's more to life than labor;
There's less to life than love.

HONORABLE MENTION
SARAH PEUGH MEMORIAL AWARD, 2011
Mississippi Poetry Society

John Osier, my Friend
(1938 - 2013)

We've seemed unlikely friends in many ways
Art lovers whose tastes were quite apart
Readers who admired such unrelated works
Writers who wrote of two divergent worlds

When each of us in turn took on the odious task
Of directing departments and a division
Of an institution whose name I quite forget, it was
With the other's blessing, care, and quiet support

In the twenty-five years we've known and shared
He and Barbara so often at our home, we at theirs,
Toasting with delicate Czech crystal glasses
They had carefully carried home as gifts

Master maker of martinis, co-conspirator
On quiet, clandestine trips to Paris and beyond
Once when I was the one "in charge" and he the one
Secretly slipping off to Transylvania, or wherever,

His parting words at the airport gate, "Remember,
I have a hundred and fifty sick days coming."
A wry smile and he was off, then, as now,
To new, exotic, strange, and distant lands.

October 6, 2013

FRENCH COAST, MURAL, OIL, 2001, 72" X 103"

Musings

In a Field in Tennessee
November First

In your father's field in Tennessee,
The small late voices of summer all but stilled,
The dull woods turned to flame
in celebration of the season of harvest
I sit, feet up, and watch you brush
the colors of this childhood land
Into a little canvas scene:
Yellow-red, rust-brown, and lingering green.

The field, beige-brown a week ago,
Is turned off-gray, bleached pale, and settles
Into the long rest, rows of stubble, bean hulls
Scattered among the shattered stalks
Covering the secret missed seeds
of the harvesting machines
Holding in toward the mother earth
the long freeze,
And the wet reawakening.

Can it be November the First?
The eye of a Pennsylvania farm boy,
Nine hundred miles from the apple farms
Tries to measure, says no,
But the man, who has seen here many times
The slow warming-on of winter, knows.

November the First. A few birds sing still
Their small and cautious songs,
The wind is warm, and the first frost not yet.
A brown wasp settles on the sole of my outstretched shoe
But cannot stay, hurries off to do his doings,
Leaving me to mine and you to yours
And the field, under the lengthening shadow
Of the multi-colored wood, to the long wait,
The sleep in peace beneath the clear blue sky
Of the shortening year.

(1980)

Al-Anon

Is this love, then?
Is this faith?
The empty bed,
The telephone ringing in darkness?
How far lies this fear
From the deep blue realm of sleep?
How cold the hands
That hold her close in dreams?
In dreams she wakes to warmth,
Whispers, touches, sighs.
                    She wakes.

1995

Out of Their Sky
(for Ed Clayton)

I drop from out the yellow desert sky
Into their dunes of heat and rolling sand;
The desert men have smoothed a stretch to land;
The Bonanza takes it lightly; so do I.
There is no place to taxi, only stop;
The sheik's young men in sand-colored drapes,
Their turbaned heads and sun-burnt leather napes,
Approach, unheeding. I kill the turning prop:
They know not what this thing of flight might do,
They who marvel and do not heed my warning;
Have I really come from Cairo in a morning?
They query close, and watch me; is it true?
An old one asks with less than deep amaze,
What did you do with the other thirteen days?

BARON, WATERCOLOR, 2008, 7 ¼' x 5 ¼"

Last Flight

The Aviator, 75, lacking a medical,
Feeling rusted on the ground,
Decides to do it all just one more time,
Keep it legal with another who is,
Retrieve the lady and roll her out,
Check her over, dust her off
Climb aboard and warm her up
Taxi her out, and take her off,
Climbing into the familiar sky,
Where she and I both learned to fly.
Go power-on and power-off,
And all the things that pilots do,
Turns and glides, dives and stalls,
Slow-flight and lazy-eights,
All with relish and with ease, while
The friend who sits and rides along
Watching with approbation, at last
Must ask the academic question:
Why do we love this flying so?
Only the steady engine replies,
Droning us back to the field again,
Easing us down to pattern height
Three precise times the field around,
Three careful landings, flaps, no flaps,
The way we all once used to fly,
The very last the best, of course,
For memory's sake, and a watching friend

On the ground to remark with pride,
"If that was the last you ever made,
It sure would be a good one."
Off the runway and up to the pump.
To cut the switches, top her off,
Thank the friend, who wanders off,
Then alone, taxi back to the hangar
Tuck her in and wipe her down,
Caress her gently, tell her aloud,
You've been a true and faithful friend
These fleeting years, and when we part,
I hope you'll like your home in Maine.
My partner there will let me know
From time to time how well you are.
So then a pause, a pat on the cowling,
Level the prop and turn away
To the rolling sound of the hangar doors
The starting car, now driving off
The airport gate, the highway home
To stow the headsets and the charts,
Make a final entry and close the log,
Gaze out the window and muse
On distant, long-forgotten skies.....
So now it's only time that flies!

(2010)

Triolet: The Time of Your Life

So soon you're old, so very late you're smart
And all the world a school more than a stage
While you would study Science more than Art
So soon you're old, so very late you're smart
You try to let your mind control your heart
Though neither can your thirsting soul assuage
So soon you're old, so very late you're smart
And all the world a school more than a stage

SECOND PLACE, DESSIE ANDERSON CAULFIELD TRIOLET
AWARD
Mississippi Poetry Society 2012 Fall Festival Competition

LABURNUM ARCH, OIL 24" X 20"

Poem on my Birthday

The morning I turned twenty-five,
Thirty-odd years ago,
I watched my mirrored coughing face
And said my thanks to chance or grace
That somehow I was still alive.

It seemed an awesome span of years,
A quarter century full,
The race half run, so little done
So little time, and what to come
But silence, doubts, and fears?

And what if I should learn to love
That self-same visage old?
Of parchment smiles, kind, faded eyes
That learn to see without surprise
Faint laureled brows above...

I fear I've not been true to chance
Through all the laughing years
When mirrored glass no more berates
Nor wrinkling smile nor love abates
The tune that calls the dance.

So here's to life and all it brings
And all these years has brought
The joyful singing, sighing heart
And all that chance could e'er impart
To the ageless soul that sings

1995

Katrina

The hurricane roils the open gulf
And one-eyed leers at the land
Her cloud-rings swirl to greet the coast
With screaming winds and sand

She gathers force; she gathers speed
Her wild winds reach the shore
Her tides have come to sink the land
For once and evermore

She means to tear apart the earth
Leave nothing in her path
Nor road nor bridge nor living thing
To answer to her wrath

The waves roll high upon the land
Crash inland through the night
Three thousand homes, three hundred lives
Are lost before the light.

Some, with cars or trucks or sense,
With late and hasty loads
Stream slowly north to safety
And block the northbound roads.

Somewhere safe beyond the storm
And long before it's done
Miles to the north before them,
A new force has begun

It gathers wire and water
And tools and food and men
To succor those it's never known
And will not see again.

The word has spread across the land
As often in the past
And reached the ears of mercy
And mercy answers fast

The trucks roll south on the interstate
Before the morning light
And some will go six hundred miles
Before the fall of night

The army trucks are camouflaged
In desert beige and green
The work trucks come in colored groups
Such as you've never seen

A hundred from a dozen states
In colors all arrayed
As if all out on holiday
For a picnic or parade

From Illinois, Missouri
Kentucky, Tennessee
Indiana, Minnesota,
Southward toward the sea.

And with their festive colors
The women and the men
Who've left their jobs and families
And won't be home till when.

They bring supplies and succor,
Tools and skills of trade
And the spirit of a people
For never long dismayed.

Some will toil for weeks and months,
Some indeed for years
And add their sweat to the ravaged land
To the salt of the sea and the tears

For something large and primal
Has struck the hearts of men
And must be shown by heart alone
That man will rise again:

The force of half an ocean
Has spent itself on land;
The force of half a continent
Returns the gifts of man.

2005

POET LAUREATE OF MISSISSIPPI AWARD
Second Place, 2006 Mississippi Poetry Society

Hymn To Science

Newton's blindness lead us on
In inquiry from dusk to dawn
Asking questions as we go
To learn what we already know.

We plod as far as mind can lead
Each idea, another's seed
To Phi Beta Kappa, PhD
Solving every mystery

Observe, measure, puzzle, guess
Arrive at an hypothesis
Test it well for lack or flaw
First a theory, then a law.

We're all know-it-alls you know;
Plato's teacher told me so
Learning's one big under-tow
What you study you already know

And where does spirit play a part
The quiet mind, the knowing heart?
Somehow something in us knows
And asks no questions as it goes.

But still we like to play the game
Discover facts, reach for fame
And at the end know with a smile
Someone's been laughing all the while

2014

War Poems

Lost in War

The German pilots all have heard
How their 109s can down our 24s:
A screaming dive behind, then up
Into that narrow space between
The tail gunner's fire and mine,
In a flash catch someone unaware
Then kill and strafe the underside at will
Until the ship, afire, goes down.
It is a brave, precision thing
Pulling G's and ready on the guns
I watch a pair together dive and rise
Like two sleek porpoises at play
The first one takes the ship below,
His guns blasting bits and pieces,
Metal and men and plexiglass;
The other one comes on for us,
But fails to get it exactly right,
A little off on the angle or the rise,
Straight into my blazing 50s,
And we go firing each at each
Until it seems that I have won;
For his guns quit while mine go on
Raking his narrow metal shroud
Where he sits dead still, staring
Straight at me with lifeless eyes,
Gushing holes across his chest,
His face as soft and young as mine,

His sweetheart's scarf about his neck
His soft-gloved hand still on the stick
Until I think the planes must touch.
His engine falters just in time
And after a moment face to face
His black ship shudders, stalls, and sinks
Away to the warm and welcome earth
The home he's risen up to guard
Now lost to him, as is this war.
He's gone to rest, and I am spared
Except those nights across the years
When I see him rising in my dreams
And wake the sleeping household with my screams.

2ND PRIZE, THE GRAND PRIZE AWARD, 2013,
PENNSYLVANIA POETRY SOCIETY

On the Death of the Late King Harold of England October 14, 1066

Struck, in the mind's eye, cast in bronze,
A figure fallen to the battled ground,
A new king down and a new king risen,
In the dust the Dragon and the Fighting Man.

At first the armored head of state
Turning within the useless helm
To watch the battle wane, and bend,
To left, to right,
Through slits of iron,
To seek the feathered shaft in flight...

And then not just the arrow in the eye,
Not just a man dead, or a king,
But the sun never sets on the Norman flag,
And falling with the stunned, shocked Saxon
Monarch of Wessex, empires and engines,
Machines of War, and a language born
To spread beyond the new king's ken,
To half the world in thrall and more,
To distant lands and battlegrounds,
And other wounds that tear the eye
And stop the heart.

1973

CASAVECCHIA CHAPEL, 1986, OIL ON CANVAS, 16" X 20"

Mississippi at Gettysburg

A seasoned, tough, and ready lot,
Fourteen hundred fighting men,
Who'd never known defeat, came to face
A Yankee force, twice their number.
Cannons and men, on higher ground
Watched the Rebs wheel into ready line,
Their fire-eater congressman-soldier,
Hero of the battle at Malvern Hill
Now a brigadier, eager as ever to fight;
"Give me five minutes," he told McLaws
"And that battery and its guns are ours."
But "Wait," was the word from Longstreet
And they waited, Barksdale's men,
Looking long at Longstreet, and waited
Until finally came Lamar, who said
"If you're ready, you may take those guns."

"That line must be broken, men!
Order arms! Load! Fix bayonets!"
Radiant, Barksdale dashed to the front
Of his old regiment, the Thirteenth
Waving his hat, white hair streaming
Like a comet's tail in the blazing heat
Of the Pennsylvania summer sun.
"Dress to the colors! Forward to the foe
Onward, Brave Mississippians, for Glory!"
And out he rode ahead, fifty yards in front;

Four regiments swept the open ground
Straight at the bursting cannons
That rent their lines, filled the gaps
Charging on, capturing both guns and men
But still not through, "Advance! Advance!
"One more charge And the day is ours!"
And there he was again in the very front,
Waving his sword at his cheering men
Who carried the day, though not the field

The "most magnificent charge of the war!"
Cost them half their men, and their general
Who dying that night in hospital,
Said, "Tell my wife I am shot,
But we fought like hell!"

2013, 2014

On the 82nd Birthday of the Navigator*
(April 1, 2002)

"Ironman Jim" is eighty-two years old
Today on his shrinking farm in Tennessee
Where he has lived by choice for fifty-three
And mined the land for cotton more than gold.
Time was, he steered his bomber to Berlin
Through the red-hot flak, the fighters, and the cold,
Saw comrades lost who never would grow old
But died ahead, beside, behind him in the din.
On D-Day from his three-mile height he saw
The greatest fleet that evermore has been
Shelling the Norman coast and moving in
In waves of blood and thunder, and in awe
Moved on, for he too had a job to do
Before his warrior days, or life, were through.

2ND PLACE, CHAD JONES MEMORIAL AWARD
Tennessee Poetry Society 2008

* Catherine's father, James A. Wright, B24 Navigator, farmer, chess champion, referred to by fellow players as "Ironman Jim."

Shiloh Battleground

(To Robert Benson)

Where a quiet holds the forest,
Oak boughs still the tree-high wind
Over painted cannon pointing
The final line for Tennessee

Iron tablets cast and darkened
On the close-clipped grass and green
Silent rising from a river
West in western Tennessee

O that I could call you, Robert,
Call to arms, to horse, to field,
Back a hundred years to battle;
Thunder sounds in Tennessee;

There to breathe with hope of victory
Sweet to die, and never see
The long defeat, the cause forgotten
By the silent Tennessee

There the enemy is waiting,
There a hornet's nest, the thicket
Bristles with his last defenses;
Foreigner to Tennessee

Gather quick defiance, anger,
Under quickening hoof-beat rage,
Tomorrow they'll be twice in number;
Grant will cross the Tennessee.

One quick final thrust at twilight
On the downward earth careening
Under oaks from Shiloh eastward
Vainly toward the Tennessee.

(1966)

On Seminary Ridge

On Seminary Ridge the cannons wait
Silent beneath the trees
Where tourists pass, and stop, and gaze
At the statue of Robert E. Lee

Behind the still of the summer wood
Mass ghosts of infantry;
The Army of Northern Virginia awaits
The command of Robert E. Lee

The cannons blast, and Lee looks out
For a signal from Stuart, who's gone;
Longstreet looks for no signal from Lee,
And the cannonade goes on.

It fills the air with battle smoke
And the wood with powder smells
And deafens the ears of the cannon men
To the screaming sound of the shells.

The hour is gone, but Lee waits on,
Till Longstreet, past all breath,
Turns to look at Pickett once,
And nods the nod of death

SEAGULL, WATERCOLOR, 17"X 14"

Then off on a march, the measured ranks
Of Virginia and Old Caroline,
With drums a-beat and banners aloft,
Parade toward the Union line...

My eyes behold this fatal field,
Where died the Confederacy;
I watch her sons march into the guns
From the shadow of Robert E. Lee.

(1973, 2010)

Love Poems

Anniversary
for CWT

Have we not run this field around
And seen in nature's eye
The glory in this golden leaf
Against this blue-blown sky?

Have we not paced together here
Afar in wind and rain
And talked of love and lost and loved
And lived to love again?

Have we not slept upon this ground
Where moonlight dreams are sown
So not one night in all these years
Has either slept alone?

Have we not wrought together here;
Both lost and won the race,
And looked the cold judge in the eye
And seen our father's grace?

November 6, 1998

Anniversary Poem for Catherine

For nineteen years of twenty-nine
To each the least has been more fine
Than all that passed before or will
When of this life we've drunk our fill

So raise with me the yearly cup
Pour more life and drink it up
So that when twenty years are done
We laugh and long for twenty-one

And may, when forty years have passed,
We still have sight that it will last
And when at last from years set free
We share at once eternity

November 6, 2000

Valentines

For Catherine on St. Valentine's Day

Lovely lady, light divine,
Shall I be thy Valentine,
Hang my blossom on thy vine,
In thy bower of bloom recline,
Take the hand which traces mine,
And meld my fragrance into thine?
Oh, give me what's already mine,
Those lovely arms about me twine,
And make my heart as pure as thine,
Pure as raindrops, rich as wine;
A love that doth my soul define,
Doth blend its lifelight here with mine;
In all the world is none so fine;
Oh, will you be my Valentine?

February 14, 1990

VALENTINE, 2014, WATERCOLOR, 7" X 11"

For Catherine on St. Valentine's Day

It seems each year at just this time
My heart's inclined to run to rhyme,
And often though it skips a beat
It never contemplates retreat
But hither sallies, love so true,
With thoughts of no one else but you,
Your face so fair, your artist's hand,
With tender touch and golden band,
Your gentle voice, your eyes that shine,
Your lips that call me Valentine.

1991

PUMP HOUSE, 1980, OIL ON CANVAS, 20" X 24"

For Catherine,
St. Valentine's Day

Twenty years ago it seems
Someone danced across my dreams
Turned my head and stole my heart
And gave my sleeping world a start:
She came and knocked upon my door
Where none like her had been before
And we both knew, that winter day,
Though neither said, she'd come to stay

1992

For my Valentine

I may not be the kind to flirt
With someone in a miniskirt
Unless she had your slender thighs
And deep dark un-averted eyes
Brown hair brushing to her waist
And lips that hint of honey taste;
I think just once before I'd die
I'd have to give those lips a try
And if that try should linger long
And longer still than this brief song
I'd ask her if she would be mine:
Oh will you be my Valentine?

1993

For Catherine, My Valentine

Now Love and Life, who run apace,
Together come to this brief place,
In concert play ancestral tunes,
Gaelic words in Nordic runes,
Console my man, delight my boy:
Sorrow lives and dies in joy;
The barrow waits the kindled pyre;
There is no death without love-fire;
And fire-clean hearts of heaven see
There is no life but mine with thee.

1994

SUNLIGHT AT PONTE DU GARE, 1978, OIL ON CANVAS, 25½" X 20"

Painted on a field trip while studying painting at Aix-en-Provence, France. Group went out to paint the old bridge, but I became more interested in the patterns the sunlight was making on my canvas and decided to paint them instead. One member of the class offered to buy it on the spot, but I knew it was for Douglas and declined the offer. (CWT)

For Catherine

If Venus ever passed this way,
Like Zephyr on a sunny day,
And found us lying on this stone,
Together two, yet one alone;
One heart a-beat with double powers,
One mind both thine and mine and ours,
One life outshining many past,
One love through many lives to last,
One will to grasp eternity
And timeless share what we must be,
Then she might wish that she might go
As one of us, and learn to know
How doubly love when thus combined
Can be more free and more refined;
She'll surely say as she departs,
Of all she's known of mortal hearts,
Of all the loves that she has seen,
That ever were or might have been,
There never was a love as fine
As this we share, my Valentine.

1995

For Catherine on St. Valentine's Day

Yes, you said, you'd be my Valentine
And spread your joy like tonic o'er my life,
You'd be my hand, my heart, my soul, my wife,
And paint the canvas that you knew was mine;
You gave in brief what you would give at length,
A sketch in dreams to stretch o'er time and space,
And drew fine lines upon my growing face,
And filled the darkmost shadows with your strength.
Today, I ask the same as I did then
But know beyond the boyish hopes and dreams
Of masterpieces forged by brush or pen
That every shared life has its better part
Of triumph, simpler, grander than it seems,
Of shouldered head, of sigh, of beating heart.

1996

GRACE, 2005, BRONZE 23"H

Valentine Poem
for Catherine

I love the way you love me:
Your deep brown eyes delight
At my arrival in your door;
Your safe, slight smile turning up
The brave line of sleeping mouth
When I but touch you in the night:
Your look, distressed if I but cough;
Your fault, assumed if I but frown;
Your guilt confirmed, if I go wrong;
Your hand that confidently paints
All that you see, all for me,
In wax or water, oil or wine,
In bright concoctions placed
Like art, designed, upon a plate.
I love the way you are to me
My every hope I dared to hold,
My star come round, my story scribed
Bold and true in night bright lines
Against the heavens of my dreams

1997

Love Lines
For Catherine on St. Valentine's Day

Like two strong strands within a rope
That share alike each twist in hope
And each upon the other's strength
Everywhere throughout their length
Turn together strong and taut
And twin partake of every knot
Which through ice or wind or cold
But tightens them and makes them hold
Thus we through years of joy and stress
Married into singleness
Have come to know as lovers must
One single strand of growth and trust
That turns and binds and holds its own
And stretches on to worlds unknown
Where there's no more of one or two
But only we: *mais suelement nous.*

1998

Poem on Valentine's Day
For Catherine

It's been a drear and heavy year
For faith and gods and lands
For hero dreams and heaven schemes
And breaking waves on sands,

For each dream flies on lead-grey skies
Through shadows forged ahead,
Nor spirits light to clear the night
Or heed the kind heart's dread,

A plan blind-spied and open-eyed
Gone wrong before begun,
A barking voice, a closing choice,
A bargain sealed and done.

Your spirit knew as mine did too
That we should turn around,
Concede the need to scan the plan
While still we stood our ground

But off we went, each other-bent
To cross dividing seas
To tread the strands of hero sands
Then home come to our knees

Where new-turned earth, a corner birth
Green marked beneath brown tree
Recalls a dark familiar bark
From far eternity.

Now new-formed ice has melted twice
And brought false show of spring
Sunned into bloom and freezing doom
Each white courageous thing

And just ere this it went amiss
On Lincoln's birthday fine
Two days ago there fell a snow
On the Mason-Dixon Line

That turned my heart from spring apart
My mind to building fires
And for a a day led me away
From the land of my desires

But soon I yearned and soon returned
To your spring-scented place
Where the daffodil and the morning chill
Come coldly face to face.

So here I stand as sure God planned
In the pleasure of your space
To seek for peace or sweet release
Or pardon from your grace.

You come at day's end as a friend,
A new pink bloom in hand,
In olden light, eyes newly bright,
Your soft voice calls your man.

February 14, 1999

Valentine Villanelle
(For Catherine)

I learn a little more of love than life,
I seek to all its double doors the keys;
I find a heaven's blessing in a wife.

Fixed in a world of fundamental strife
I come to mix my visions with my pleas;
I learn a little more of love than life.

I come to know and trust the surgeon's knife,
And feel the sense of earth beneath my knees;
I find a heaven's blessing in a wife.

I march in time to swirling drum and fife
And have my search beyond the seven seas;
I learn a little more of love than life.

I build a house and fancy as housewife
An artist-spirit swinging 'neath its trees;
I find a heaven's blessing in a wife.

I bank my fires and feed my inner life,
I sense my spirit soaring as it flees;
I learn a little more of love than life,
I find a heaven's blessing in a wife.

February 14, 2000

BARKLEY, 2012, WATERCOLOR, 16" X 20"

For My Valentine

Have you not been my valentine,
My summer rose in winter's day,
And turned to blue the skies of grey,
And filled my heart with schemes of May?

Have you not been my valentine,
My fairy child, my ocean pearl?
Have you not been my love, my girl,
And set my heart and soul a-whirl?

Have you not been my valentine,
Shared my fancied world with me,
And by confining set me free
To all your boundless liberty?

Will you still be my valentine,
Today as you have been before,
And add this day to those of yore
That love might last forevermore?

Will you still be my valentine,
To feast in years the plan divine,
To cast your future days with mine,
And toast the world in love's red wine?

Will you still be my valentine,
When love is old, and more than kind,
And travel with me as I find
That all that's left is left behind?

February 14, 2001

Valentine, 2002

Catherine, if I made a wish, and do,
It would have to be for more than you
Could give with painted hearts and flowers,
Cards and music, candlelight, and wine.
Though I might have such just desserts
On thirty more occasions such as this,
I'd ask instead your hand in mine,
A smiling face set toward the stars,
Into the weather and the wind,
Beyond another thirty years,
A prayer said to grace my table,
Cheery cheeks from morning walking
Thoughts shared deeper than the talking,
Dark brown eyes behind closed lids
On pillows piled on our joint bed,
And Love awake throughout the night,
Oh these many years. Then morning light
With all the world a sunrise, every space
A golden call to walk again in joyous pace
And peace of heart, oh grace of grace!
In short, I have all you could give,
All that love and life can live,
And yet I yearn by heaven's door
That you might give me more, and more.

NEW OCEAN # 2, 2014, OIL ON CANVAS, 22" X 32"

For Catherine, my Valentine

In the year just past, I love you well
On highland crest, on ocean swell
Beside the sea, in high blue air
In morning light, awake, aware
In sunset walks or dark of night,
We scan the stars, and all is right.

In the year that starts today
I love you more than I can say
I love your hands that strive to mate
The works of art your dreams create
The same artistic hands that grace
With care the contours of my face
The heart that loved, and loves, and will
Yearn most of all my life to fill,
My health, my wealth, my ample store
My every dream and many more.

So what have I to ask of thine
That is not now already mine?
And what have I to give to thee
Since thou are more than part of me?
In every part and in the whole
You live already in my soul.
So I must ask of God and you
That all our highest dreams come true
The ones that see us hand in hand

In far or in familiar land,
That see our works together grow,
See minds and spirits all aglow
In health and joy another year,
Another, and another year,
Until these first faint thirty-one
Seem but the day when we'd begun.
And if allowed to stay with you,
As in every prayer I do,
I thank this God for thirty two.

February 14, 2003

There Came a Knocking

There came a knocking on my door
When I was young in days of yore
And all of life I'd known before
That day was changed forevermore.

Across the room and down the hall
I hurried, not aware at all
That suddenly the sky might fall
In answer to that summons call.

I turned the knob and smiled to see
A good true friend who'd come to me
And brought a fairy, light and free,
And she glanced up and smiled at me.

Her hair was long and dark as wine
Her shoulders small and square and fine
Her aspect earthly yet divine --
And when she smiled the smile was mine.

I knew that smile should never be
More that a glance away from me
And somehow God had meant that she
Should share my soul eternally.

I laid my heart at her fair feet
And saw that fairy smile repeat;
Oh, to taste those lips so sweet,
There could be no greater treat.

Her brown eyes dark with hidden fire
Held faint hint of sweet desire
Like the stroking of a lyre
Or the singing of a choir.

Their instant flash of deep delight
When first I came into her sight
Brushed away my deep heart's night
And set a thousand wrongs a-right.

Then each twinkling eye a star
Shining with more truth by far
Than ever any doubt could bar
In silence said, So there you are.

That day was many years ago,
But yesterday, as true loves know;
The friend has gone, as friends will go,
And left my love with me to grow.

February 14, 2004

For My Valentine

If love were light and light were love
You'd shine as bright as those above
I know in fact that this is true
Because, my love, that's what you do

The sun by day, the moon by night
Are both eclipsed by your true light
The stars by night, the sky by day
Behold a light more bright than they

You shed your light upon the earth
You bring delight and love and worth
And I in turn have come to see
The light that God has sent to me.

2005

WITH MY COLLIE, WATERCOLOR, 10½ x 13½

For Catherine, my Valentine

The very day you came along
And turned my story into song
Of sweet confusion and of love
The morning bells began to ring
My waking heart began to sing
And I heard music from above

The first time ever your eyes met mine
Your soul proclaimed that I was thine
All in a flash your friend, your man.
They glanced away, but it was done,
In time to come we would be one;
That was the day my life began.

The first day ever you smiled at me
It filled the state of Tennessee
And swelled the sky and set me free
It made my heart to leap and fly
Though reason could not tell me why,
And drained my soul of aught but thee.

The first time ever I took your hand
I pictured there a wedding band
Though years would pass before the time
When it was real, and yours and mine,
And love arose to quell the dark
That evening walking in the park

The first time ever you shared my path
I knew it was no god of wrath
That sent you here by His design
But One who measures Love alone,
Who leads us each one to our own
And fills us each with light divine
As mine is yours and yours is mine.

2006

For My True Love on Valentine's Day

They called this world a vale of tears
This valley of delight
And I suspected through the years
That they just might be right

I'd known enough of loneliness
Of love engaged and lost
And little reckoned anything
Could make it worth the cost

But you came from your mountain-top
And shone upon my plain
Dissolved the mist and gave a kiss,
Never to leave again.

You offered me the gift of love
You placed it at my door
And promised it would never fade
If I would keep it pure.

I'd known that love could never last
'Twas a momentary thing
But when I looked into your eyes
I then knew no such thing.

You saw that I could do no wrong
You were in fact most sure
And I beheld the same in you
Whose love was right and pure

That day was half my life ago
All my life, in fact,
All things measure from that day
When love was born intact.

2007

DAYDREAMER, 2013, BRONZE 38"H
FIRST PLACE, PEOPLE'S CHOICE COMPETITION, 2015
Meridian Museum of Art

Thank You
(for Catherine)

Allow me lady, to give thanks
For the gifts which you outpour
For all the things you do for me
Enough ten times and more

Thank you for the morning sun
Which you alone make rise
For the silver moon and evening star
Which you bring to my skies

Thank you for the light of noon
That shines forth from your face
To catch my unsuspecting days
And fill them full of Grace

Thank you for the many gifts
You give me day and night
For breakfasts in the morning
And love by candlelight

For paintings painted just for me
And sweet meals made the same
For every time in every day
That you call me by name

For all the years that you have shared
And blessed them as they passed
For every moment from the first
Until the very last

For the gentle touch of your soft hand,
Your breathing in the night,
For the soft voice in the darkness
"My love, are you all right?"

Yes, my love, I am all right,
With all our yesterdays entwined,
With dreams we have and still shall have,
And all that's yours and mine.

St. Valentine's Day, 2008

LITTLE DANCER, BRONZE 8½"H

For Catherine

I love you for I have no choice,
I sing of you or have no voice;
I tell this love to fit the season,
Follow my heart, lose my reason

I love you for the years we've known
The joys and gains while love has grown
The trials endured that still try now
Your faith alone that shows me how.

I love you for you bear me well
And carry me, though none can tell,
Your quiet calm ignoring fears
Your bravest smiles in place of tears.

I love you that your faith can be
What nurtures you and carries me
And for the grand enduring art
That springs to life in your sweet heart

I love you in your heart of hearts
In all your deepest dearest parts
The mind that knows, the hands that mold,
And paint in pigments pure as gold.

I love your soul which sees us through
To all that dreams and faith can do,
Your steady strong unfailing love
Known but to me and God above.

St. Valentine's Day, 2009

For Catherine
My Valentine

It's come around again, that time
When spirit new informs the mind,
Commands the heart to sing again
Of gifts of life and love, now when
My ship's come in, my sky turned blue
All because you told them to;
Each time I turn this well-worn ring
It makes my spirit want to sing
Each time I view your loving face
It makes me thank God for his Grace
For fate that brought you to my door
For love which stayed forevermore
For all our joys and everything
That makes me want to laugh and sing.
Thank you from my singing heart
For playing out your faithful part
In life and music, home and art,
For all the years you've made me whole
With joy and laughter in my soul.

2010

Valentine, 2011
(for Catherine)

I'm asking for the 40th time
Or could it be just thirty-nine
Since I was young and in my prime
And boldly wished you to be mine
And you became my Valentine

As I recall those early years
Filled with trials, triumphs, tears,
The thrill I felt with your first touch
Your smile that made me oh so much
The dreams it launched as smiles will do
The warmth that made them all come true

So now I hope as I did when
That if I dare to ask again
You'll smile with joy as you did then
You'll say that I'm your prince so fine
And you my Princess Valentine.

2011

For Catherine, My Valentine
(a Villanelle)

I knew that forty years would never do
When first your brown eyes stole a glance at mine
To share such love of life and live anew.

A knocking door; in came my friend with you
Have you a minute? Chills ran down my spine;
I knew that forty years would never do.

Of course, I said, come in, and sit, please do
And you, fair lady, please, the pleasure's mine
To share such love of life and live anew.

You stayed, we talked, and everything so new
For me, like sunrise, visiting a shrine
I knew that forty years would never do.

From that day on we're best of friends, we two
Blessed in health and hope and joy divine
To share such love of life and live anew.

When I awoke this morning next to you
And saw my precious love and Valentine,
I knew that forty years would never do
To share such love of life and live anew.

2012

HONORABLE MENTION, BARRON AND DESSIE CAULFIELD
MEMORIAL AWARD
Mississippi Poetry Society 2012 Fall Festival Competition

Two Paths Converged

Two paths converged in Tennessee
On a once and distant time
Your path came from your front door
And my path came from mine

My path had roamed both near and wide
To your path quite unknown
But each one sparked a living fire
As each drew nearer home

The artist's heart and gifted hand
Caught the poet unaware
And left him at a loss for words
Though he knew his soul was there

The paths then straightened out to run
For years in parallel
And though they rarely were conjoined
Everyone could tell

The poet's words ran clear and true
The artist's eye grew deep
And sculpted many a wonderment
For a world that seemed to sleep

There now no longer are two paths
But one path intertwined
That brings the world two pilgrims
In soul and heart and mind

Two roads intermingled
Until they are but one
And the single road goes farther
Than the two could e'er have done.

Valentine's Day, 2013

February Poem
for Catherine

February again, and here am I
Ready to praise you to the sky
But with a record to maintain
I can't repeat some old refrain
I have to make it new as new
Or it will never do for you
So it's a challenge every time
To put sweet love in matching rhyme
And work with courage, not with fear
And hope anew for just this year
Heart may fear but spirit knows
Work improves as pressure grows
Before the situation gets much worse
I'd better write some charming verse
And try to woo you with some lines
Outshining all the valentines
Composing poems just for you
Is far the happiest work I do
But still I know I must endeavor
To be to you more true than clever
And pray for love that lasts forever.

2014

Valentine 2015
for Catherine

When I was young and knew it all
I fell in love spring, summer, fall,
I was so mature and wise
I knew that it was all a guise

So-called love was just Romance
Though happily it gave a chance
To learn some lessons out of school
And dance the dance and play the fool

To break some hearts and lead to ends
That were the envy of one's friends
And then pass on when morning came
To other loves and other games.

But then one fateful winter day
When I was not inclined to play
A friend dropped by, and with him you
And suddenly the game was through

From that day on and every spring
Love became a different thing
Slowly stronger and more sure
That it would flourish and endure

The lessons came on one by one
And were weathered every one
Even when we weren't prepared
For every challenge now was shared

And as the scope of love matures
And turns each wish from mine to yours,
We ask for years without an end
My lover, teacher and best friend.

Songs

Railroad Tracks *

Railroad tracks a-layin'
On that flat black delta land
Reachin' down to Jackson
And on to Lou-sianne

    But I ain't gonna ride that train
    I ain't gonna ride
    I ain't gonna ride that train
    I ain't gonna ride

Rode that train to Texas
Down to San Antone
Half-way to California
Rode it half way home
(Refrain)

Cotton fields a-growin'
Right up to the track
If I ever ride that train
I know I won't be back
(Refrain)

Railroad tracks a-windin
Down along that river shore
If I ever go a mile
I'll go ten thousand more
(Refrain)

1971

Railroad Tracks

Douglas Taylor

1. Rail-road tracks a-lay in' on that flat black Del-ta land, Reach-in' down to Jack-son, and

Refrain

on to Lou-si-anne. I ain't gon-na ride that train, I ain't gon-na ride,

I ain't gon-na ride that train, I ain't gon-na ride.

Verse 2:
Cotton fields a-grown', Right up to the track,
If I ever ride that train I know I won't be back.

Verse 3:
Rode that train to Texas, Down to San Antone,
Halfway to California, Rode it halfway home.

Vesre 4:
Railroad tracks a-windin,' Down along thast river shore,
If I ever go a mile, I'll go ten thousand more.

* At certain times songs have come to me, much as poems some-times do, and I find myself first singing them, then writing them down. *Railroad Tracks*, occurred one hot summer afternoon when I was driving on Mississippi Highway 3, in an open-air Volkswagen "bug." There was a railroad running parallel to the highway, with a freight train going about the same speed, and as the song came to me I began singing it. This went on for several miles, until I had three verses and a refrain, which I sang over and over in order to remember the words. Because of my work I had several tape record-ers on the back seat, so at one point I reached back and brought one to the front, took the microphone in hand and sang through all three verses, complete with chorus each time. The greatest diffi-culty came later, with the play-back, trying to hear my voice over the recorded noises of rushing air, the VW engine, and the train. (CDT)

Sing Me A Song

Sing me a song of that time of the year
When the trees are bare and the skies are clear,
When the wind blows cold and the end is near,
Sing of that time of the year.

Sing me a song of December then,
Of the leaves in the wood and the loss of a friend,
Of the long winter night that will never end,
Sing me a song of a friend.

Sing me a song of the snow in the air,
Of the eye of a bird and the words of a prayer,
Of the song of a man when a man's not there,
Sing me a song of the air.

Sing me a song of the spring to come,
When the flowers will bloom and the streams will run,
When all of your friends will be there but one,
Sing me a song of the sun.

1972

Sing Me a Song

Douglas Taylor

Sing me a song of that time of the year, when the trees are bare and the skies are clear, When the

wind   blows cold   and   the   end   is   near,   Sing   of   that   time   of   the   year.

Verse 2
Sing me a song of December then, of the leaves in the wood and the loss of a friend,
Of the long winter night that will never end, Sing me a song of a friend.

Verse 3
Sing me a song of the snow in the air, of the eye of a bird and the words of a prayer,
Of the song of a man when a man's not there, Sing me a song of the air.

Vesre 4
Sing me a song of the spring to come, when the flowers will bloom and the streams will run,
When all of your friends will be there but one, Sing me a song of the sun.

The Troubles Waiting There

Born to lie among the rushes
Born to cross the parted sea,
Born to lead us to the Jordan
Born a slave that would be free

But oh the troubles waiting there
Oh the troubles waiting there
In this world he could not stay
For it all should pass away
But oh the troubles waiting there

Born into a humble stable
With Angels singing everywhere
Born to save this world from darkness
But oh the troubles waiting there

Oh the troubles waiting there
Oh the troubles waiting there
In this world he could not stay
For it all should pass away
But oh the troubles waiting there

Born into this world my brother
Born to sorrow, pain, and care,
Can you see across the river
To a valley green and fair.

The Troubles Waiting There

Douglas Taylor

1. Born to lie a-mong the rush-es, Born to cross the part-ed sea,

Born to lead us to the Jor-dan, Born a slave that would be free. But

Chorus

1. Oh the trou-bles wait-ing there, Oh the trou-bles wait-ing there; In this

2. 3. No more trou-bles wait-ing there, No more trou-bles wait-ing there; In this

world he could not stay, For it all should pass a-way, but Oh, the trou-bles wait-ing there.

world we can-not stay, For it all shall pass a-way, No more trou-bles wait-ing there!

Verse 2
Born into a humble stable, With angels singing in the air (everywhere)
Born to save the world from darkness, But oh, the troubles waiting there!

Verse 3
Born into this world my brother, Born to Sorrow, pain, and care
Can you see across the river, To a valley green and fair?

No more troubles waiting there
No more troubles waiting there
In this world we cannot stay
For it all shall pass away
No more troubles waiting there

1973

Greeting Card Verse

Lighthouse Notes

(Verses from a series of 24 cards, each with original watercolor, historical note, and verse, 2001)

Set A: The Carolinas

A1: Hatteras Lighthouse, North Carolina

> A hundred years and more stand I
> Where surf in thunder rolls,
> And breaks through ribs of ghostly ships
> Lost on the Diamond Shoals

A2: Ocracoke Lighthouse, North Carolina

> I am Blackbeard Island light
> The eldest on this strand,
> This narrow, battered outer bank
> Between the sea and land.

Hatteras Light, Cape Hatteras, NC, 2001, watercolor 7½" x 11½"

A3: Bodie Island Lighthouse, North Carolina

> The sun sets over Pamlico
> And leaves the world to me,
> And through the night I spread my light
> Afar o'er land and sea

A4: Old Charleston Lighthouse, South Carolina

> My light gone out, my people lost,
> My island washed away,
> I stand on neither sea nor land,
> And guard Fort Sumpter bay.

LIGHTHOUSE, BODIE ISLAND NC, 2001, WATERCOLOR, 7" X 11"

Set B: Florida & Georgia

B1:   Pensacola Lighthouse, Florida
(on Pensacola Naval Air Station, home of the "Blue Angels")

> I stand upon this inland height
> And guard the narrow bay;
> I feel the thunder in the sky
> And watch the Angels play.

B2: St. Simon's Island Lighthouse, Georgia

> History hides in the tower walls
> While we climb the winding stair
> And weary at the top arrive
> And breathe the salt-sea air

B3: Tybee Island Light, Georgia

> Through war and wind and earthquake
> And shifting coastal sand
> I've sent my light through storm and night
> To tell of the port at hand.

B4: Ponce de Leon Inlet* Lighthouse, Florida

> 'Twas no site for man nor light
> To share their shifting roles,
> Midst malaria, mosquitoes
> And sneaking Seminoles.

*Mosquito Inlet Lighthouse; begun 1835; delayed by malaria and Seminole Indian threats. Name changed in 1920s to help local real estate sales.

Set C: International

C1: Biloxi Lighthouse*, Mississippi

> I lift my ancient iron light
> Beside this ruffled bay
> Where tropic nights and traffic lights
> And modern pirates play
> (2002)
> I stand within a present
> Well rooted in the past
> Of shipping lanes and hurricanes
> And haven't seen the last
>
> I've stood my ground since '48
> Mid storm and war and test
> And like as not the bravest lot,
> Were those who manned me best.
>
> Now on this coastal highway
> So battered and storm tossed
> From motor cars to casino bars
> I still may guide the lost.

(2013)

HONORABLE MENTION, FRIENDSHIP AWARD 2013
Mississippi Poetry Society

BILOXI LIGHTHOUSE, WATERCOLOR, 7" X 11"

* Mississippi's only surviving light, built 1848, of cast iron; stands in middle of four-lane highway (US 90) on the Mississippi gulf coast, now heavily populated with casinos.

C2: Yaquina Head Light, Oregon

A strayed ship on a fog-bound sea
Left me stranded here,
Yet four hundred thousand people find
My "lost" light every year.

(Intended for Cape Foulweather, 4 miles north, but ship
left build- ing materials at Yaquina Head, now focal point of
Yaquina Head Outstanding Natural Area.)

C3: St. Catherine's Light Tower, Isle of Wight, England

There is a place twixt then and now
Where dim eyes plainly see
How I stand bright by day, by night,
And cast my light to sea.

(Built 1323, out of service by 1785)

C4: "La Vieille,"* Isle of Sein, Brittany, France

The old one clings to her rugged rock
To guide the men of Sein,
"One fourth of France," as they set sail
And to light them home again.

LA VIELLE, BRITTANY WATERCOLOR 7½" X 11½"

*"The old Lady," at Pointe du Raz, "the far rock," off the very western coast of France. The Isle of Sein was the first to rally to the Free French in 1940. 130 men sailed for England that June, 29 of them never to return. General de Gaulle called their little force "one-fourth of France."

Set D: New England

D1: Boston Harbor Lighthouse, Massachusetts

> Still one last light, and that the first,
> Of all in this wide land,
> Shares her space with human grace
> And knows a keeper's hand.

America's first lighthouse, erected in 1716. Only U.S. lighthouse
that is still staffed (by act of Congress) and not automated.

D2: Burnt Island Light, Maine

> Two beacons guide thee, mariner,
> Our sheltered bay to find
> But the first light is a Cuckold
> And the second seldom kind

(At entrance to Boothbay Harbor; visible only after clearing the
rocks at Cuckold's Light)

D3: Nobska Light House, Woods Hole Neck, Massachusetts

> The red man ceded to the white
> This site thus set for me,
> Where still I stand upon the land,
> For who can cede the sea?

(on land granted by the Indian Job Notantico to Jonathan Hatch of Suckanessett, Massachusetts, December 30, 1679.)

D4: Fire Island Lighthouse, New York

> Has new light broken in the west
> For those in Europe's night?
> Give me your lost, your tired, your poor,
> And guide them by my light.

(the light for which trans-Atlantic steamships set their course when leaving Europe)

Set E: Maine

E1: Portland Head Light, Maine

> Hie me to thy haven, light,
> Beneath thy rocky lea
> As thou hast seen me hitherto
> Safe to the open sea

E2: Pond Island Light, Narraguagas Bay, Maine

> Some stand upon the outer rocks
> Whilst others bridge the bay,
> And some, their lights unwanted,
> But stand there in the way.

(built 1856; privately owned since 1934; not a functioning light)

E3: Bass Harbor Head Light, Maine

> On these hard rocks, by this cold sea,
> This small but rugged light
> Stands by the way to Blue Hill Bay
> And shines out red at night.

E4: West Quoddy Head Light, Maine

> East is east and west is west
> And neither one is mine,
> Where sea and shore meet evermore
> And know no other line.

(on the easternmost point in the United States, just west of East Quoddy Head Light, Canada)

Set F: Atlantic Canada

F1: Louisbourg Lighthouse, Nova Scotia

> To ship or shore, forevermore
> Her signal flashes free,
> The second light upon this height
> By this cold northern sea.

F2: Prim Point Lighthouse, Prince Edward Island

> Beside this bay on Edward's Isle,
> Through bitter cold and night,
> A hundred fifty years and more,
> I've turned my ice-bound light..

F3: Peggy's Cove Lighthouse, Nova Scotia

> The tourists take my summer sun
> Like wild birds in their flocks;
> Lone ships washed in winter ice
> Stand off these mortal rocks

F4: Tiverton Light, Digby, Nova Scotia

> The fisher turns to scan the sky
> And pulls a weather oar
> Then spies the spark that through the dark
> Will see him safe ashore.

Christmas Cards

(Done annually, but often all sent out, hence this limited selection.

> *O Child of woman, Child of God*
> *O Day-Star in the dead of night*
> *O glory of the new-born age*
> *O gift of love and hope and light!*

2003

> *Let all the world rejoice and sing*
> *Hosanna to the new-born king*
> *And let heart hear beyond all sight*
> *Angels singing in the night.*

2004

> *May all the joys of Christmas-tide*
> *Fill your house and heart with love*
> *May every gift you ever give*
> *But spread the gifts of God above.*

2005

> *May all the joys of Christmastide*
> *and all the glory of God's Love*
> *Surround you and your family*
> *With bounteous blessings from above*

2006

BLUE MADONNA W/DOVES, WATERCOLOR, 5" X 7"

Hail the child of glory
Hail the child of light
Hail the ancient story
Of angels in the night

2008

An angel of the Lord appeared,
We heard the shepherds say
And Lo, the middle of the night
Shone brighter than the day

Fear not, fear not, the Angel said
Give off your fears and hidings
Behold I come from God above,
A bearer of glad tidings

A child is born of Abraham
Of David's line descending,
And of his peace and earthly reign
There shall be no ending

2014

Welcome Home Cards

Welcome Home I

Happy Traveler, welcome home,
To rest in warmth, and cease to roam,
For though from hearth we travel far
'Tis home informs us who we are,
And when, through charting wind and stars
We reach the door we know is ours,
Oh, the joy it can impart
Unto the mind and to the heart

Welcome Home II

Where'er the mind may wish to roam
The heart in part remains at home;
And the weary wing doth doubly rest
In its own sequestered nest.